Emblems

poems by

Carol Nolde

Finishing Line Press
Georgetown, Kentucky

Emblems

Publisher: Leah Maines

Editor: Christen Kincaid

Cover Art: Photograph of Georgina Taylor Stephenson and her son James

Taylor Stephenson, the author's grandfather and great-grandmother, 1901.

Author Photo: Tamara Beckwith

Cover Design: Elizabeth Maines McCleavy

Order online: www.finishinglinepress.com
           also available on amazon.com

Author inquiries and mail orders:
Finishing Line Press
P. O. Box 1626
Georgetown, Kentucky 40324
U. S. A.

Table of Contents

For Frank and the family

I

Emblems

Her satin slipper crushed the ruby
berry hidden in the grass.
One wild strawberry's sweetness
pressed into the satin of her shoe
and with it the June sky and fragrance
of berries and hayfields rolling
below the church into the valley
so when she spoke of the day
the slim shoe held in her knobbed
hand, she pointed to the stain
as if to say, "This is how it was."

Mornings I'd watch her wrap her bunion
before she'd step into stretched, misshapen
shoes, then tie the laces and her apron
before she'd begin the day.
"We sang in the choir together."
Rolling out pie dough, she still sang
and rocked grandchildren to sleep
their heads against her rumbling breast.
"We married where we met."
I tried to picture her in satin shoes
in her father's carriage climbing the hill

to the clapboard church that glistened at the crest.
Horses and carriages lined the fence;
friends and family, the pews. All waited.
With one hand she lifted her skirt to clear
the wheel, the other pressed into her father's
palm. Poised as if to pirouette,
she paused to ready herself for the step
and when her slippered foot touched the earth,
it found the berry.

A Marriage

They'd been married sixty years when he noticed
she'd gaze distracted, wondering
if she'd put baking powder in the blueberry pancakes.
Then she forgot names, faces,
then how to button her dress
so he took care of her
bathed and dressed her
and every Sunday bundled her into their old Chevy.
They crept along backroads that crisscrossed the farmlands
Aunt Rose's eyes barely above the window frame.
The day they caught me raking leaves from the ditch,
Uncle Willy rolled the window down.
We talked and Aunt Rose smiled and nodded
her wrinkled hand a claw on the door
her bright eyes blank behind glasses.
I thought of their farmhouse cradled in the fold of hills
that were their hayfields and pastures,
the barn full of cattle, the house full of children.
Now the barn long empty
the girls in New Jersey, Pennsylvania, Alaska
the one who stayed behind, twenty years dead of cancer.

They said Uncle Willy nursed Rose for weeks that winter
sat by the bed listening for her breath
and when he knew the end was near,
he climbed into the hollow in the bed beside her
and held her in his arms.

On Our Anniversary

All night on the hill our two lights
have burned, yours in the barn and mine
here where I'm lost in Hardy's moor.
Now in the dark the barn door
slides shut. You're whistling Mozart—
the rung you'd cut for the chair must fit.

When you enter, the Sunday puzzle tucked
under your arm, your presence fills the room.
I press into its warmth as I close
the window against the August night.
All summer long we've absorbed
country stillness, bent in the garden

or rising to gaze at the hills,
felt our bodies slow to the diurnal
turning of the earth, held the sun
at dusk in our watch from the porch,
the way the ear holds a note
that fades so slowly it doesn't know just when it dies.

In the deepening dark we walk the meadow
your hand on my shoulder the same that trembled
when you pressed me close in dance
and your whispered love warmed
my ear. Now as you speak
of painting the barn, the boy's
enthusiasm flashes and your eyes hold
the girl who's hidden from the world.

My love, I fit into the curve
of your arm as sure as when I drop
back into the pond, arms outstretched
to sky and trees, knowing the water
will cup my weightless body, carry me
as long as I trust its strength.

Promise of Flowers

for Frank

Warm days drawn to the porch,
they dream on the steps, seeing in the garden
the early green's promise of flowers.
Their voices languorous in the spring sun
speak of the planting the man
has begun now that the sun has warmed the earth.

His wife knows the feel of earth
between his fingers and the beds by the porch
are even in winter dreams of the man
by the look of his eyes when he speaks of the garden—
a grey sky suddenly brightened by sun—
as if in its light he quietly flowers.

In the middle of winter, it's the promise of flowers
and the sure and steady spinning of earth
closer each day to the warmth of the sun
until the slant of light on the porch
signals it's time that work was begun in the garden
that makes winter's dark pass for the man.

The drive that pulses in the blood of man,
the need to bring something to flower,
has the man on his knees by the garden's
edge where he brushes a leaf or a crumb of earth
from the shoots of crocus that rise by the porch.
Then he sits on the steps with his wife in the sun.

He knows that his work depends on the sun
and the rain—so much is out of the hands of man,
but daffodils soon will nod by the porch
and beside them a carpet of crocus will flower
purple and gold on this plot of earth
that he has made brighter by planting his garden.

They mark the months by the blossoming garden.
In May the red tulips cup in the sun.
June, roses and clematis, trellised from earth,
above iris and peonies rise to the man
and his wife, who savor the fragrance and colors that flower
in the beds that he's planted beside the porch.

The circling earth marks the days of a man;
too soon the last aster in the garden sun
will flower and fade beside the porch.

With Him

He'd left the house without her.
Probably by now halfway home,
she thought, so when she reached the street
they always took for their return
barely breaking stride she decided
to reverse their route.

Like a film on rewind
the houses, trees, fences flicked
by in new order. She hadn't noticed
the gradual decline of what was now an uphill climb.
Then she saw him. Was it joy she felt
just knowing his blue jacket moved toward her?

Expectant, as the night in the supermarket when
the bent frame and white hair ahead
said it was her father, long dead.
She'd hurried toward the retreating back until
at the aisle's end he turned.
Then she'd feared she would cry out her loss.

Now her steps quickened as her eyes embraced
the blue advancing figure and as they met
she turned, fell into pace beside him.

East Hill View

"The health of the eye seems to demand a horizon. We are never tired, so long as we can see far enough." Emerson, Nature

Summer evenings we linger until dark
strolling in orchard or fields
held by power the view wields
until we can only hear the dog bark

in the meadow below ours.
Fall twilights, brilliant but brief,
in silence so deep, drop of apple or leaf
sounds, suspended in day's last hour,

we gaze across valley at woods that yield
to house and barn and road,
land cleared by ax and stoneboat's load.
The rock now walls that edge the fields,

mowed smooth. Our hill mirrors theirs—
the same high plain eroded
and glacier rounded, perhaps, encoded
with the same message as pairs

of twins repeat a pattern.
But our hill's more woods, farms grown up in trees.
Ours is not a view to please
a farmer. He would spurn

this giant's cheek unshaven, this land back
to blackberry vine and brake
that needs clearing to make
room for house and garden or farm. No lack

of will keeps our land open, so
from porch, garden, or orchard seat
we can see the horizon and sky meet
and the work of the farmers we follow.

Windfalls

We've never owned a gun and if we did
who would shoot? But when we see our beans
nibbled down to stems, the killer instinct
controls all reason. Death to deer
who jump our fence, ignore the hubcaps strung
on string across each row or human hair
we saved all winter tacked on posts along
our garden's edge. But after harvest of all
the deer had spared, we watched from kitchen window
two young bucks who'd come for apples under
our trees. They browsed in mist that hugged the ground,
the world all grey before the sun. So many
windfalls they did not finish one before
they moved on to the next.
On slender legs they lightly stepped, raising,
at times, their antlered heads to listen—still
except for tails that flicked white flags above
their chestnut backs that just last spring were dappled
white, their branching antlers, only buds.
I raised my hand to tap the pane, but stopped.
One nudged the other's flank—that's all he did
to start a little fun. With antlers locked,
they danced in rings, then pulled apart like schoolboys
to eye each other for a better hold.
They charged. Through the window I heard the whack
of bone on bone. But neither hurt, they wheeled
again for blows. This time they rose on hind
legs to spar, but broke and turned their separate
ways— brothers, back to apples. Then one heard
or sensed us there, for quickly as they'd come,
they disappeared.
I looked for them each morning, but they did not
return and soon the apple crop was gone.
November days when rifles crack, I wonder
if they're safely lost in woods or are
their bodies held for flight in sight of guns
about to fire? Then draped on hoods of trucks,

the tongues that knew the taste of apples, hanging,
they'll travel speeds they could not comprehend.

The Dark

Death leaped from beneath a stone ledge,
grabbed a leg. The struggle
for freedom sank the fangs
deeper into flesh—then a still
gathering of strength, but the snake's jaws
widened and like a leather glove eased
over the roundness of the toad until only
its eyes stared out as if to catch
a last look before the dark. Then
as the forked tongue flickered, the mound that stretched
the skin's checkered brown undulated down
the snake's still length.

Like the suicide's empty chair
the stones bear no mark to say
the dead was here.

Betrayed

They'd built the nest beside our door before
we'd come with all our human noise. Too late
to move away—the eggs already warm
beneath the breast that rested there until
a hand let slip the screen that banged an exit
or an entrance. Then she'd flutter up clucking
her anger or dismay, impossible
to say, from the vantage of the line or roof
until we'd gone away. We took to using
a different door to not disturb her nerves.

We'd circle the bush to see her snuggled in—
her head tipped back, her beak upraised
and staring back her black, unblinking eye.
Soon she knew we were not worth her fear
and let us water flowers beside her bush.
She did not move except sometimes to stand
as if to stretch her legs from so much sitting.

The day the eggs were hatched we gathered round
the bush like relatives who press their faces
against the glass to see whose nose or eyes
or chin will bless the tight-shut face.
Each morning marked their progress. Opened beaks
first lined the nest. Then heads appeared
and soon whole birds that burst the bounds
onto the branch. That's when the cat attacked.

The parents' cry drew us too late to save
them all, but like benevolent gods we lifted
one into the nest and beat the cat
from those still fluttering on the ground. The screams
above our heads drove us away who could
do nothing more than say the saw about
the red of tooth and claw and hope somehow
they understood how helpless humans are.

All About Crows

Crows have little beauty—plummage, solid
Black, a call that's loud and raucous, melodic
It is not! Known to pillage corn,
Three hundred thousand plus were killed
By conservationists' command in one
Enormous blast. But did you know that crows
Will mate for life? That young help raise their parents'
Or brothers' broods? And crows whose young have flown
The nest will chip right in and feed
The hungry young? So family size around
A nest may even reach fifteen! One female
Banded before she left to nest a mile
Away returned each Friday afternoon,
It would seem, to hang around the folks!
So all that squawking that we hear from trees
Along the golf course edge is nothing
More than clan all gathered round to cheer,
Perhaps, a baby's flight or play a round
Of drop and catch the twig or tug of war
With blades of grass. Sometimes, it seems, for fun,
They swing below a branch suspended upside
Down. And if you haven't guessed, they love
To talk. Their vocal skill in saying "caw"
Provides some twenty distant calls
While quiet, intimate family speech
That sounds like "rattles, gargles, growls, coos,
Squawks, and squeals, and plaintive oo-oo's"
Carry meanings we can only guess.
We're even told that crows of East and West
Have different accents! Now I find I listen
To crows' cacaphony and hear in noise
Familiar strains of family harmony.

The information in this poem is based on the research of Dr. Donald Caccamise, Dr. Carolee Caffrey, Dr. Lawrence Kilham, Dr. Kevin J. McGowan, and Dr. Cyndy Sims Parr as found in the article "The Too-Common Crow is Getting Too Close for Comfort" by Jane E. Brody in *The New York Times*, May 27, 1997.

Tattooed

For weeks we watched the owls. Their nest, the angle
of roof between the barn and shed. At first
all four could sit in sun, a speckled row
of down, but as they grew the number fell
to three, then two, the rest in dark behind.

We called our friends to see—our barn had owls!
We cheered their flight from roof to tree, but wings
of only three were strong. One sat forlorn,
if that can be, and only ventured to
the edge, it seemed, to watch.

                         One day the nest
was empty. We found him down below a heap
of feathers. Through the downy breast, his heart
tattooed against my palm. I pushed him back
into the dark of nest. Again he fell.

For days we tried to heal his hidden wounds
with food and finger strokes and gentle words.
All failed. His eyes unblinking, blank, not wise,
not comprehending us or fate, at last
closed. I buried him behind the barn
in moldering leaves as light and brown as feathers.

On His Own

At dusk we waited—almost able to measure
the passing season by the sun's earlier setting
further west. Light was his clock
and as it left, his head appeared above
the window frame, a black lump that hunched
over the edge (I swore that once I saw
his toes curl around the frame) poised
as if to survey the scene before he dropped,
but as in dreams of falling, propelled his way
up and out long before he hit
the porch floor and floated over the rail.

We called him "he" because he was alone—
he suckled none. Droppings from only one
fell below the window or streaked the stucco.
Despite the mess, I felt somehow privileged
he'd chosen shelter within our walls. Some
people put up boxes to lure bats,
but ours just found us. I remember
when I was a child, a bat, blinded by light,
battered against our kitchen ceiling until
my father, swinging wildly, hit him,
then carried away the tiny body, lifeless
on the back of a broom. Only recently I read
mysterious deaths by rabies are caused by bats.
A girl camping with her family died untreated
because no one knew she'd been bitten.

I think of our bat clinging to the wall of a cave
probably somewhere in Virginia where so many winter
and wonder where he'll live when he returns
to find his home filled in. We'll probably
see him in the orchard along with all the others
who skim above the trees, silhouettes against
a darkening sky, but we won't know which
one he is, and like a child once
they no longer live under the family roof,
he won't be ours.

Going Home

Nearing the road that once led home
an impulse urged the wheel to turn in the old
direction, follow the rain between folds
of fields once farmed, now woods. Only the stones
stacked to mark boundaries spoke like tombs
of the work of those who tried to hold
the power of nature back, knowing control
was never theirs. The homestead loomed
as it always had, a ship in the sea of dark.
So I could almost believe if my tires crackled
over cinders from winters of ice, a barking
dog would rouse the dead who lived in the ramshackle
house, and someone, a coat draping his head,
would step from the porch, offer warmth and a bed.

Before acid rain

had emptied the lakes, the men fished.
On the way home they'd stop at Riley's for a short one.
Laughter and whiskey breath filled the kitchen
where they'd dump their buckets into Grandma's deep sink.
Here I was drawn by the sound of tails smacking porcelain.
Eyes stared that maybe only an hour before had seen
the lure bobbing on the brown surface of Camel's Creek.
Pickerel, bass, catfish, perch from Silver Lake,
Pike's Pond, Birch Ridge, ponds that dot the map
and pock the land where glaciers moved and melted.

Grandma would line the drainboard and sharpen her knife
before she spattered iridescence over the pages
of yesterday's <u>Tribune</u>. Careful as a dressmaker opening a seam,
she'd run her blade up the fish belly and scrape the flesh clean.
At the enamel table she arranged the bowls for dipping
first in flour, then egg, then cornmeal, before they were dropped
into the bubbling black skillet. At supper when teeth broke through
the crusty brown to the sweet, white flesh beneath,
the tongue responded as it had for centuries when fish
from these same ponds were roasted over open fires, a stick for a spit.

Obsolescence

"Old barns are as obsolete as the manual typewriter in the computer age."
John Berdo, a seventh generation farmer, *The New York Times*

The land seems barren when a barn disappears.
On the hill opposite ours where Kimball's fell,
my eye fills the blank that for a hundred years
or more was a family farm. There I knelt
in a field to pick wild strawberries, so ruby
ripe my fingers stained with their essence. When trees
had taken back those fields, the barn stayed
though it seemed to grow smaller and darker as it decayed
on the hill opposite ours before it fell.

Half the country's wooden barns are lost
whose hand-pegged beams once held
cattle and horses and hay forked into lofts.
Livestock and machines too large for a barn
are housed today in metal sheds. No fear
once real that fire will devastate a farm.
The land seems barren when a barn disappears.

Storm

Snow clung to your denim jacket like the smell
of cattle as I kissed your cold, unshaven cheek.
Across the red linoleum, your boots leaked
rivers. I laughed as you began to tell
of tunneling to the stable. The stove had cast its spell
as you rubbed chapped hands. Though wind shrieked
in the chimney, wood shifted and the house creaked,
it seemed there was nothing that warmth could not repel.

Snow outlines the field's stubbled rows
and frozen tracks, plasters the trunks of trees,
edges the barn's weathered red to enclose
all in white. The sky does not relieve
the threat of night that's setting out to reclaim
the earth, of drifts against granite obliterating your name.

Fox Hunt

on a painting by Winslow Homer (1836-1910)

Half-buried in snow, Homer's name rises
black on white in the painting's left corner.
At the center a red fox sinks, belly deep
in the drift, one paw upraised in labored flight
from black beaks hovering so close
the snow silent air beats with their cries.
Hunger has driven him to the edge of the dark
sea that foams against gray rocks.
Everything is buried but a wild rose bush
one bough above the drift, bent
with ruby hips the wind will whip until they drop.

Comfort in Stone

The stone bridge still arcs the stream
That swept all others in its flood,
Loosed from land all that stood
Too close to its banks, it seemed.

Our bridges made of steel bent
Like stalks in the teeth of a mower,
Pulled down by the current's power,
Cleared away by energy pent

Too long within a narrow bed,
Surging up as if to show
All of us we did not know
As much of bridge building as the dead.

The dinosaur of bridges stayed
Its grey legs planted in the bones
Of the muddy stream that roared and foamed,
Its stones hewed from the land and laid

By men who built as if what they did
Was part of some important plan,
Their work the measure of a man,
To stand in judgment of the life he lived,

Swiss Germans who farmed the banks
Almost a hundred years before.
Its triple arches built more
For the future than ours that sank.

Stone on stone they'd laid the piers,
Pointed prows to break ice floes
And three arches to withstand the blows
Of the swollen stream we'd come to fear.

Its strength outlasted those hands, now bone
That reared its flanks against time's wear.
We who gather by its side to stare
Find comfort there in stone.

II

The Beginning

The end does not announce itself.
Sometimes a word or gesture suggests the ominous,
but though the rules aren't clear, the cards just dealt,
the players in a Wessex tale, even if dubious,
begin. So Daddy drove our old Chevy
to weekly meetings for men returned from the war
while we waited in the car. Once in awhile we'd see
the class pass outside the barn, their scars,
if they had any, invisible. They were here to learn
the latest methods for raising livestock and crops,
veterans in a new field. Allaying concerns,
the expert answered their questions, so at Mullally's, our stop
on the way home, Mother and Daddy made plans,
laughing over mugs of beer, confident in their hand.

Not Like Dick and Jane

The odor of our wool mittens drying by the stove
rose with the dough spilling over the bowl's rim,
mingled with scent of cinnamon and clove from spice cake.
My mother's yoked print apron white with flour
stretched across her belly rounding below her breasts.
Her stubby fingers shaped even rounds of dough,
pressed them in threes like clover leaves in greased tins—
such precision present nowhere in her life,
the product of her hands, not her mind, which beat against
the panes of light, shrieked like crows over torn flesh.
But Saturdays the cookie jars, bread box, and cake
tins swelled with bounty she'd stirred and shaped and baked.
If only we could have pressed our heads against her aproned
belly, brushed the flour from her cheek to plant a kiss.
Instead when our toes warmed, we shoved our feet into boots
still damp, pulled on steaming mittens,
and raced into the cold.

She Preserves

She might have been Lady Macbeth returned from the dead
king and the gilded guards as she stood at the sink,
her hands streaming red rivers
along her bare arms.

Instead Mother peeled
and dropped beets into steaming jars,
pressed their roundness into the curve of glass.
All that we didn't eat in summer, she preserved—

bushels of beets scrubbed, boiled, and slipped
of their skins, and the greens washed leaf by leaf
then thrown into a roiling kettle
to settle limp in hot jars.

Each day of harvest, a different color
and shape to dip and peel, pit and press,
stir and sieve or slice until the pantry
shelves sagged with the weight of her store.

Mother worked centuries old spells
from formulas found in a stained brown book
for "Minnie's Mustard Pickles," "Mrs. Eggler's Relish"
until even her hair smelled spiced.

Perhaps in incantations over the pot, she whispered
fear, drove her anger down the knife
that sliced into the chopping board,
contained her confusions in the order of jars

that lined the pantry shelf each night to cool.
When we'd cleaned the garden and the orchard floor,
the jars emptied last winter stood full
ready for the storms we knew would come.

When the window held only winter dark
I'd leave the kitchen's light and heat
and follow a plank into fragrant damp.
Alone in the heart of earth and stone

I'd find the string that snapped into view
corn-yellow, pea-green, tomato-red, the amber
cheek of peach pressed against glass,
the ruby currant, amethyst elderberry, garnet raspberry

that could transform bread. When I'd hear her cry,
"What are you doing down there?"
I'd snatch a jar and bound upstairs
holding all that was left of summer.

The Gathering of Women

Once a month at three, before the children
had tumbled from the bus to break the silence of a house,
the women of the hill gathered. They'd slip out of aprons
and cotton housedresses, bathe and powder
and smooth silky dresses over hips
before they'd shut the door behind them.
They'd walk along the red shale road,
a linen handkerchief tucked in their sleeves
or between their scented breasts, toward the cool,
shade-darkened parlor that waited.

By the time the children arrived, they were deep in a story
nodding over an illness or death or sighing
of betrayal over a second cup of tea
and in their center, platters of cookies and cake.
The children, wedged between mothers and grandmothers,
stayed silent until the story's end.
When the platters circled again, there was laughter
as the women marveled over the lightness of the cake,
the crispness of the cookies. Repeating recipes, they carried
their dishes to the sink and vowed to meet again.
Children in tow, they hurried down the road
toward the meal that needed getting on the stove,
the table to be laid for men soon up from the barns.

Lost World

How he would have laughed to think a day
was set aside to show the way a farm
is run and who would even come, who
had time or interest. No need to chronicle the daily.

Even the curious would not want
a predawn tour to milk the cows,
shovel the drop then wheel into wind
to a manure pile frozen behind the barn.

No, better to arrive in afternoon,
catch a glimpse of cattle lined in stanchions,
the barn clean, the farmer free for the visit.
Better summer than winter, a warm breeze,

fields green, machines gleaming in the yard.
So forty years after most farmers had sold
the homesteads, watched trees overtake
the land their great-grandparents had cleared,

"Down on the Farm Day" began, part
of an August weekend to lure
tourists to dying towns that needed no cure
when stores sold what farmers needed.

The farm on display is run by a boy I knew,
an athlete with body now bent as a tree
that somehow has sprung from rock.
In the creased leather of his face, I see

the road the years have followed and if I hold
the hand I shake, palm up, run
my finger over his callused life-line,
the cracked skin of his thumb

I am holding my father's hand
that winter nights he worked with lanolin,
first into back, then palm and especially
the thumb's tip that each day opened raw.

With My Father

He must have found peace in the flank
he pressed his head against, the steadiness
of the stream he sent into the pail.

The cats waited for him to stand
before they ran to the dented pan
they knew he would fill each milking.

The calf he was trying to wean seemed to feel
the calm in the hands holding the pail she butted
before letting herself drown in her mother's nectar.
For me it was the way he listened, accepted
the weight of anything I couldn't carry.
Even my mother who had no use

for the way we'd talk would sometimes shout,
"Go tell your father."
In winter when the size of the rooms couldn't

hold us both, the barn was my refuge.
In its warmth it was almost possible to forget
the wind except for the way it rattled the window,
shifted the snow on the sill.

The Christmas Village

In the dark room, lying on our stomachs,
we looked into the life of the village
lit by the rainbow tree
and a yellow glow through cellophane panes.
Your voice led me along cotton streets
to a pond where a skater fluttered frozen
and watching behind pines, deer unafraid
of the human world or the polar bears
that lumbered along the tree's base
where skiers were caught in the thrill of descent.

Your words wove the village story
in which a girl with my name skied and skated
and awaited Santa, warm inside a glittering cottage.
The glass globes that weighted the branches
caught but could not hold our reflections.
Unlike the mirror lake forever frozen,
the celluloid deer never slain,
the bauble that slips from the bough
shatters into silver slivers.

The Homestead

for my father

The morning our first calf was born,
you came from the pasture pulling her, wobbly
on a rope. "What will we name her?"
"Janie," I said, pressing my cheek against her coat rough dried.
The barn then was notes on paper
that each night you nibbled a pencil over.
Mornings just one milk can glinted near the road
and the chickens laid eggs under bushes,
not yet in the coop you would build.
The farmhouse with blue ball lightning rods
stood sturdy as the maples that lined the drive,
saplings great-grandfather staked when he built the house.

I'm older than you were when you took the office job,
nine to five, a sure paycheck, and whiskey before supper,
the homestead in the hands of city people who did not know
how dark the nights could be so far from town.
Now the barn roof caves in onto the floor you poured
and smoothed until the level told you it was true.
Windowless walls bulge waiting for heavy snow.
Blackberries and poplars grow in the fields
you cleared with ax and stoneboat
and the hemlocks you planted around the porch
tower toward a window where a curtain flaps surrender.
I stand at the edge of the wreck
like a child poking a dead animal with a stick,
afraid some life may stir, the front door fling
open and someone forbid me step closer,
so I circle the house and barn with a divining rod,
searching for the spring that once could fill your cup.

Connected

"Farmhouse for sale" the billboard blares
then lists the towns where anyone with money
can find a perfect place for country living.
So Uncle Len's and Matt's, then Willie's sold
to people who had no way of knowing the life
and death that happened there in space they now
began to rearrange to make their own.

Antique shops, boutiques, and galleries line
the street where once a week farm wives
shopped for groceries at Cousin Jenny's store.
The farmers went to Beck's for whatever they couldn't
find at home: bins of nails, nuts,
and bolts, boots, hats, overalls, liniments.
If it wasn't out, John found it in the back.

Men have scraped and painted Jenny's and Beck's,
hung signs: "Tanning Salon," "Mountain Antiques."
The windows are clean again, the walks swept,
and pots of flowers bloom beside the doors.
Shoppers can find quilts to hang on walls,
egg pails painted white for magazines,
and milk cans with decals to decorate a doorway.

Uncle Willie's porch no longer sags,
his rocker replaced by white wicker. Here
warm evenings, he and Aunt Rose had sat
to watch fireflies signal above the fields.
The house is air conditioned now and the owners,
their faces lit blue by the t.v.'s beamed messages,
no longer are isolated between the earth and sky.

"Bright Light at Russell's Corners, 1946"

"To Make a World: George Ault and 1940's America"
Smithsonian American Art Museum, May, 2011

Ault knew the dark of country roads
how suddenly a road can bend, send a car floating
free out over a lake like Icarus
before his descent, swallowed without a trace.
So the artist was drawn to the bright light at Russell's Corners,
the way it illumined the side of a red barn in need of paint,
signaled the need to slow down on the right-angled macadam.

Ault's widow told of the way he ordered his studio
put everything in place before he could begin to work,
perfect as the white building in this painting that hugs
the road's edge, its clapboards narrow and straight.
Opposite, in silhouette a derelict split-rail fence
surrounds a dark field that needs mowing.

Power lines, lit gold, score the sky, emphasize
the dark of a country night without moon or stars.
Only the light at Russell's Corners keeps
the stranger's car around the hairpin turn
known to locals, but the light beckons to all who travel
an otherwise dark road, reminds them that maybe
cattle are bedded in the barn and inside the house someone sleeps.

III

Land of the Heart

Paintings of Adriaen Coorte (active 1683-1707)
National Gallery of Art

*"The poem...can be a message inside a bottle, sent out in the not always
secure belief that it could be washed ashore somewhere, sometime,
perhaps on a land of the heart..."* Paul Celan

The texture is so exact that we can see
the cut ends of the asparagus starting to dry
and the individual xylem appear.
Fibers of the frayed cord around
them are visible against their white flesh.
Light from an unseen window illumines
wet red currants that hang from the table's edge,
silvers the tips of their dark velvet leaves.
Wild strawberries heaped in a Chinese bowl,
chestnuts strewn on a cracked stone ledge,
seashells, peaches, gooseberries.

Nothing is known of the artist who signed and dated
these small still lifes except
he sold them in Zeeland for a meager sum.
Today in the gallery, crowds press to study
the simple objects caught in the light of a dark world.
No words tell the painter's thoughts.
But in the translucent beauty of gooseberries,
the perfection of the strawberry blossom that will not last,
we can only guess what drives an artist
back and back again is desire
somehow to get the vision right.

In the Artist's Hand

Mary Cassatt exhibit, the Museum of Fine Arts, Boston

Cassatt's pastels, chalks of no particular
brilliance, broken, not what one would expect
in a master's hand, encased and labeled, a curiosity
below the portraits.
                              Such a meager store
to capture the sheen of leg-of-mutton sleeves
so that we feel the yellow silk beneath
the child's hand, the peach roundness of the cheek
the mother's face is buried in. Which sticks
of color could have blent to fix the shimmer
of red-gold hair and hint of brows
above the eyes so blue the whites appear
blue too, the gaze assured safe
from the noise and notice of the world? The moment's private
when the mother's lips have met her child's cheek,
the child pressed against familiar warmth
that glows pink to red along the lobe,
exposed by the sweep of hair into a bun,
a roundness complete as the sleeve encircling the child.

As a writer's words lying flat and black
sometimes will rise above their ordered lines,
her chalks illumine a world that defies a frame.

A Lost Duchess

"If you could choose a painter for your portrait,
who would it be?" he questioned over lunch.
They'd seen so many women caught by men
on canvas, she paused, her fork mid-air and looked
into his laughing eyes and wondered how
he'd like to see her done.
                            Perhaps as pink
cheeked Artemis in bosom baring gown
of rustling silk, one ribbon tied about
the whiteness of her throat. Her bow, the only
sign that she is goddess of the hunt.
"With the children?" she asked.
                            "It's up to you," he smiled.
She saw herself a Sargent duchess—languid,
the arms of her diaphanous gown like wings
along the damasked sofa back encircling
her children, dressed in white, her ringed fingers
caressing golden curls against her breast.

"I think I'll have the portrait just of me."
She knew the way she wished to be remembered
and who could capture truth about her best.
She saw the background dark, its details spare,
the light oblique upon her figure, plainly dressed,
her hands at rest upon her lap, blue ridged,
red knuckled, unadorned. Her eyes, like opals,
catch the light. In them, the painter reads
her life and leaves it for the world to see.

Her husband leaned across the table, "Well?"
Although she feared her choice would disappoint
because he loved the grandeur of the past,
she softly said, "It must be Thomas Eakins."

Mother and Child

on a painting by Cecilia Beaux (1863-1942)

Gowned in black, she sits in profile, her head
bent over her child, who rests against
her breast. He's tired from play or maybe half
asleep just risen from a nap. Perhaps
she's been away. Are those her gloves on the table
near them? He's missed her comfort all day.
Her eyes seem closed, the way a purring cat's
see all through slits. Her arms encircling him,
cannot contain the sturdy legs that dangle
from his dress of ruffled white and might
without a moment's notice send him sliding
from her silken lap. For now, he feels
the steady rhythm of her breath, her fragrant
warmth beneath his body pressed to hers.
There with her, he dares to stare at us,
who stand outside the private space they share,
and at the world that he will leave her for.

Now a Mother

It's the way my daughter's arm encircles
her baby, whose bare back bends
toward the sand and waves that lap
at her mother's feet, her tiny
buttocks resting on the arm beneath her.

It's the way my daughter's body leans
toward the water, wanting the child to feel
the pull of sand and sea,
but only so much,
as someday she'll urge her
to greet an admiring stranger,
but hold her hand.

It's the way
their flesh meets
arm, buttocks, hand
the way I still long to touch the back
bent above the child,
want to hold them both,
knowing the bond that joins, separates.

At Auschwitz, In a Display Case

Pale blue, handknit in the finest wool,
the kind of baby sweater seen only in exclusive
shops, but here among these artifacts,
I picture the young woman who sat by a window to knit.
The light touches her hair, the rows of stitches
that grow above her rounded belly, or maybe
it's her mother, longing to hold a child after many years.
The sweater, she feels, makes the future real.
She can almost see the blue eyes like her daughter's,
imagine the sweet scent of the body against her shoulder,
the neck she will nuzzle.
                              When word comes
that they must leave, she helps her daughter pack
and in bold letters labels the suitcase *KIND.*
Is the sweater folded inside or did they struggle
to put the tiny arms in sleeves, a layer
he will need against the coming cold?
And when the guard commands, "Form two lines,"
does she offer to hold the child because she knows
the old and very young are sure to die?

Kind, the German word for child

Civility

Today thousands of people converged on the lawn
for Mozart. After the last gong
of the summoning bell, an expectant silence fell,
so ears could accept the first note.
Under puffs of cloud adrift in blue
the heart opens as it cannot
under crystal chandeliers gone dim
above dark rows where pages rustle
and coughs strain behind cupped hands.
Here, two ten year old boys weave among blankets.
One with finger to lips checks the other, already silent,
before they settle under a yellow umbrella.
Even the two year old in pink-checked pinafore,
playing with her mother's sandals, is part of the silent story
each blanket or cluster of webbed chairs could tell,
but differences here are subsumed. We attend the piano
that sings to winds and strings, gives voice
to questions no words can still.
The music tries and in the space it fills,
we listen.

Varanasi, Night Ride

The boatman rowed us over the river
famous for the dead burning on its banks
the corpses that sink into its dark
then rise to lift an arm or hand
curled toward the boats and votives
floating on the sacred road.

He kept us a "respectful distance," he said,
from the relatives carrying litters draped in gold
down the steep ghat toward the water.
Logs rolled from piles that line the bank
become a pyre for the body's ascension
through gray air and the odor of burning flesh.

Over the black water we sent votives.
No one spoke as we neared the shore.
Past the hungry eyes of a legless beggar,
children's open palms, we climbed stairs
toward rickshaws and the men who would carry us
weighted by all we had seen.

Vultures

Determined to return, one circled the field.
The other mounted the barn, a weather vane
that fanned black wings to balance in the wind.
Though driven from the dead, they did not call like crows
but silent sat or soared in wait. They knew
their beaks had marked it theirs. They'd tear the flesh
from bone until they'd rise to beat the air
above the skull and rows of razor teeth
they'd leave to bleach in sun.

Tiger Hour

Rathambore, India

No fear in the inexperienced, the young deer
grazed their way across the plain in morning peace.
But when a few antlered heads suddenly rose
even the peacocks stood at attention,
followed their gaze beyond the watering hole
into the tall grass. High-powered binoculars
could not perceive the presence that for a moment held
all. Then drawn back to the familiar, they fed.

For over an hour we watched, spoke in hushed
voices, if at all, waited with them
for what seemed the inevitable. Would the morning end
in flight or would one young or old and frail,
who cropped sweet grass in early light, fight
to live? Like a gun sounding the start of a race,
a samba deer snorted an alarm that scattered life
away from the parting grass where Death emerged.
One swipe of its terrible paw could have felled
any but the strongest. But speed or luck saved all
and Death lay down, for the moment thwarted.

Mysteries

Her baby in one arm, the other she extends, hand cupped,
then raised to press her fingertips against her lips.
On the temple road, clad in white tunic and white turban,
a supplicant casts himself full length on the pavement.
At each step he drops and rises, drops and rises.
Workmen on scaffolds wash the Empress' marble tomb.
A pool doubles the glistening dome, white against blue
as ox-drawn mowers perfume the air.

Only men accompany the dead, descend the river ghat
to carry the litter into the purifying water of the Ganges.
In the light of pyres, the golden shroud glitters.
Each day the mother and baby stand in diesel exhaust.
She raises her cupped hand toward a bus window,
then presses her fingertips against her lips.
The man in white labors toward Rathambore.
He believes he must reach the steep on his knees by holy day.

Thousands of men worked over twenty years at the Emperor's command,
raised a monument of perfect symmetry, fashioned with inlays
of marble, yellow and black, red stone from Fatehpur Sikri.
The air in Varanasi hangs heavy with smoke.
The sick and the dying have come here to bathe in the holy river,
send flower-laden candles adrift on the current.
The mother extends her cupped hand, then presses her lips with her
fingertips.
Even protected in white gloves the penitent's hands bleed.

Horus' Eye

So many forties' films begin on trains—
The camera focuses on a woman's white legs
crossed beneath a smart suit, maybe
a veil falling from a hat set at an angle
to cover thick lashed eyes above
a full, dark mouth we know must be red.
Opposite, a man barks words and smoke
between a narrow line of lips—his eyes
slits from smoke or stealth take her in.
In truth, I'm hatless in a flowered skirt beside
my husband, who also doesn't look the part,
but here we are skimming across the desert.

The tick of the rails, steady as an old projector
on rewind, takes us past the black and white reel
to ancient times that flicker in the frame of our window,
but the women who kneel on the banks are real.
Not posed in prayer, they bend to the Nile
to dip the clothes they rub against rocks
while a shadoof lifts a bucket for white robed
men who feed the green they've planted in rows
along the banks. Sometimes a donkey
driven circle after circle turns
a wheel that raises river to field,
Archimedes' modern way to water.

We are headed south against the current
to the Aswan Dam that does not allow
the north flowing Nile to flood its banks,
instead transforms its force to light.
As the train moves forward taking us back
toward the river's source, I stare
at people bent over work
that has not changed though centuries have passed.
They only glance at the silver snake that slides
along the rail and at our faces framed in glass.
They do not know that film winds behind
my eyes, records the silent mystery of their lives

so when our plane rises above the desert
brown, I will look down into the muddy river
racing between strips of green and unreel
a past that lies beyond all living memory.

Suzhou, Two Views

I.
In the Nobleman's Study
         "In heaven above there is paradise, on earth...Suzhou..." Yang Chaoying

"Beauty Within Reach" he named his retreat.
Peonies' sweetness perfumes its dark cool
above the garden and pool where carp glide.

When thought does not allow the pen to glide,
he can walk in sunlight, leave this retreat,
let his mind drift with the water in cool

shadows of rocks washed, creased by rivers. Cool
mind returns, still as a butterfly glide,
open as peony in sun. Retreat.

Pen glides over page. Shadows, cold, retreat.

II.
In the Silk Factory

In the silk factory, rows of women
stand hours before bubbling troughs. Whirring fans
the only relief from the concrete's heat.

Red hands reach into the seething stream's heat
where cocoons bob, release thread the women
guide onto spinning reels. No painted fan

will grace small hands worked raw. To speak with fans
demands time, not factory speed and heat.
Cooled showrooms hide the labor of women,

heat in silk's sheen, a woman's folded fan.

Sahara Dark

The tent zipper's squawk and my circle of light
intrude on the black silence. I hold my breath.
Listen. No sound. I move in stealth
toward a tent I know is there though my sight
cannot confirm it. In such a night
I can believe the universe would weather
the loss of human life, even the death
of our galaxy and the billions beyond. Our matter is slight,
four percent, I've read; the rest is dark,
unknown for now and possibly forever.
Disoriented and lost in the cold and dark, I shiver
but stop to marvel at the shower of stars that arc
above my head. The rest is mystery mass
I will never know beyond this bliss.

IV

Memorials

We were away the night the car crashed
at the end of our lawn, but the glass shards
and twisted bits of metal we raked,
the carnations tied to the trunk shorn of bark
told some of the story. Today pink plastic
flowers and a white tee shirt are tacked
to a telephone pole on the route I take to work.

I think of Mexico where flowered crosses mark
every curve. They seemed part of a fascination
with death like the wax effigy of Christ,
full-sized and bloody in a glass coffin,
the chest weeping, the flesh extruded
and the tomb open to the public that displayed
a procession of skeletons propped along the wall
their tatters of cloth still clinging.

Thirty years ago my brother fell asleep at the wheel.
No one decorated the concrete with flowers.
And though I wondered, I never asked
which road, which bridge.
Not knowing helped.
I try to imagine the highways and backroads of the world
all flowers and mementos restored
and those that were never placed,
this thin layer of time and space
suddenly crowded, filled with testaments of loss.

The Burning

for my mother

The coroner handed her the jacket
folded and wrapped in brown paper.
"I thought," he said, "you'd want to save
his letters"—orange wool her heavy
thread had bound to black.
She hid the package in the spare room—
only the dreaded coffin ahead,
the words of comfort to wade through.

After she'd emptied the last casserole,
washed and returned the last dish,
she climbed the stairs to the cold room
to hold the parcel's weight in her lap,
pluck at the cord she knew she had to cut.
Blind fingers read the wool
that last had warmed the body
she'd held within her womb.

Then folding the jacket stiff with blood
back in its paper pocket, she carried the bundle
down the stairs, stopping only at the stove
for matches. She did not feel wind whip
her robe, the snow enclose her slippered feet,
but when she reached the metal drum
behind the barn and struck the match,
she wept to watch flames lick the dark.

Unclaimed

At the Florence Foundling Hospital

We swaddled our first born child
in soft, sweet smelling flannel.
Waving her arms and legs, she would look up
from the center of the cloth diamond
as her father folded her into its warmth,
placing one point over her legs and stomach
drawing the other two over the first
tucking them firmly under her body.

I see her in the Della Robbia reliefs
above the hospital's colonnaded porch,
terra cotta cherubs, porcelain-white
looking down from sky-blue roundels.
Most have lower bodies swaddled, though some
have wiggled free, the blanket dropped back
to reveal the sex. Arms opened wide,
they accept all who ascend the steps.

I wonder if a mother who entered here raised her eyes
and saw their smiling beauty or was she blinded by grief,
by fear that this would be the last she would see
trust in her baby's eyes, feel the warmth of his breath
against her neck. Soon she must leave,
place him within the horizontal wheel
that would rotate him away into the building.
Then she could leave unseen.

But first she must record his identity.
How carefully she must have tied the ribbon around his ankle,
so returning, she could say, "The child with a green ribbon,
'Eduardo' embroidered in white."

Here in a case, parents' last gifts,
identity affixed to the child they hoped to reclaim:
a silver bell, a glass scent bottle,
a strand of beads, a cross with red stones.

The Search

For Jonathan on the Appalachian Trail on his Twenty-first Birthday

This summer my son and I are finding ourselves.
In the Georgia hills 2,000 miles of trail before him,
he begins.
I sit before the computer, its light white in the dark room.
The past and all the words I cannot live without
lie heavy
not neatly stowed as in his pack
maps needed razored out of books,
foods dried, measured, bagged.
I do not shoulder my pack,
weigh the worth of what's inside,
decide the need, the use of each,
but like the turtle what's there's attached,
so my ascent is slow.
His will be too, he tells me,
till legs and back from days' demands
respond to mind.

On mountaintops grey with mist,
he'll hoist his pack as morning breaks.
A notch, a gap,
a knob, a bald,
a ridge, a creek,
a spring his aim.
Gooch Gap, Shuckstack, Clingman's Dome
mountaineer named.

I sip my coffee, check my watch, imagine him in those distant hills
five million steps from Georgia to Maine—
The first day he walked to school alone
I stood at the kitchen window
waving each time he turned to wave
waving after the corner house had swallowed him up.

Now under Georgia sun, sixty pounds of food and gear strapped to his back,
he struggles over boulders
towards hardwood groves,
wild flowered balds and pink tunnels of rhododendron.
My words start across the page and stop.
For every hundred I write, seventy-five crossed out.
We are each lost in our wilderness.
But at day's end, the supper steaming over the single burner stove,
the aching body stretched on firm earth,
the ink black on the white page.

Note: In 1948 Earl Shaffer was the first person to walk the entire 2100 miles of the Appalachian Trail from Georgia to Maine. At one point he counted his steps and calculated two thousand to a mile, or about five million from Georgia to Maine.

Finisterra

Where the sea hurls itself against land's end
a church rises from rock, a beacon,
not to sailors, but to those they left.

Through its thick closed door, the roar
of sea and wind drowns the human voice,
rocks the rafters where votive ships sway.

Knees turn cold on stones that line the aisle;
above bent heads, the tiny vessels
voyage, heavy with hope or grief.

Dream of Spain

If I were a wave lapping Coruña's rocky harbor,
maybe I'd catch a glimpse of you hurrying to work
down the pink, palm-lined sidewalk,
but it wouldn't satisfy me any more
than the vibrations over air that register
your voice in my ear. No,   I'll be a cat,
one of dozens among the stones that feed
on water rats and fish scraps tossed from boats.

In my disguise, I'll be   Marmalade,
the tabby you mothered when you were ten,
who taught you the pain of separation.
Reincarnated, I'll crawl from between the stones,
startle your memory in my orange and white coat.
You will bend, croon to win my confidence.
I will sniff your open palm, press my warmth
against your legs, weave a circle around you.

Surprised, you'll pick me up, call me "Kitty."
and I will nuzzle your ear and neck knowing
the scent beyond soap, sure that it is you.

Ex Voto

When my body seemed no longer a stranger
I wanted to give thanks. If religious,
I might have traveled to Mexico to a saint's shrine
hung a replica of my skin draped like Jason's fleece
to join the arms, legs, hands, feet
that dangle around the marble stele.

If Frida Kahlo had been freed from pain
perhaps she would have painted an *ex-voto*
followed a familiar pattern: in the top third
a saint floating over the body of the sick,
and along the bottom the cure rendered in words,
a paean rising from joy in health.

Music's Power

on watching the documentary Alive Inside

His grizzled head rested on his chest.
No touch or soft words could encourage
him to lift his eyes, view the world
he lived in for ten of his ninety years.

Washed, dressed, medicated, barely alive
until the day they fed Cab Calloway's voice into his ears.
When the familiar strains flowed into his body,
tugged the marionette string burrowed in his neck,

his head jerked up, his eyes widened, bulged,
and his mouth so long only an opening for food and drink,
moved and from a hidden spring, a stream welled
and Calloway's nonsense syllables danced into the room.

So it was, again and again that music found
a conduit to the world inside and those who did not smile,
suddenly snapped their fingers and sang and the lame
lifted their hands and feet, moved to the beat of their youth.

And I began to understand why when I was desperately ill,
Hank William's voice, country music my father played,
songs I had not heard in years,
made me feel safe, helped me heal.

Making Bread with Jonathan

Begin by crumbling yeast into warm milk.
It is morning—snow glistens on the forsythia bush.
When the yeast bubbles, the bread will rise.
My son measures flour into a glazed white bowl.

In morning sun, snow glistens on the forsythia bush.
He dusts his hands on his apron and waits.
He's measured flour into a glazed white bowl.
Cover it to keep the dough warm.

He dusts his hands on his apron and waits.
In the branches chickadees cascade showers of snow.
He's covered the bowl to keep the dough warm.
Think of friends as you knead, I say what I'd been told.

In the branches chickadees cascade showers of snow.
Mid-morning, he's amazed as dough rises over the rim.
Think of friends as you knead is what he'd been told.
By noon browning bread perfumes the room.

We gaze at the dough rising over the rim.
Thump the loaf to see if it's done.
It is noon and bread perfumes the room.
I have never known such peace.

Thump the loaf—it is done.
When yeast bubbles, bread will rise.
I have never known such peace.
To begin crumble yeast into warm milk.

Roberta's Rhubarb Cake

She photocopied the recipe she'd baked for over forty years,
handwritten on typing paper, "Very Good" scrawled at the top.
Each time she baked it, she noted the occasion,
"Nan and Pop's 58th anniversary," "Jeanne Erdman's funeral."

That's when I tasted it, a spiced coffee cake
rich in butter and cinnamon, moist with sour cream
and learned with surprise the bits among the chopped nuts
were rhubarb stalks "cut into tiny squares."

Recipe books entice the baker to replicate the glossy photo
but this recipe drew me into another life
when "Rob and Betty visited 5/15/75"
and the spring when "Nan harvested rhubarb" and "Mary Ann stirred."

Birthdays, anniversaries, reunions, funerals noted and named,
moments dark and bright, a legacy of joy and sorrow
when the tongue, perhaps rendered mute, was given power
to press a sweetness against the palate, express what words could not.

Recipes

My father-in-law worked his way across the Atlantic
and landed a job as sauce chef at the Waldorf.
His gravy recipe begins: "Roast thirty pounds
of veal bones." His Christmas stollen:

"Pour twenty-five pounds of flour into a tub.
Mix with six pounds of softened butter."
The letters on the yellowed paper round, bold
as the commands, remind me of the hand

that squeezed butter through sugar and almond paste,
the fingers, so large the diamond he wore on his pinkie
fits my husband's ring finger. The recipes
were cut when he died to fit our diminished size.

From childhood, Mother's pound cake, calls
for eight eggs and a pound and a half of butter.
On the farm there was always a bowl of cracked eggs
in the refrigerator and the empty cake box to fill.

I study the shape of Mother's letters, the product
of Palmer practice books, on the index card
she'd slid into a plastic sleeve of the ring-binder
she gave me when I married. The glue that held it dried

and the recipe stained and frayed after it found
its way into my envelope labeled "sweets."
Here are chocolate cookies in Grandmother's hand,
her final "t's,"not crossed, but ending in a flourish.

She would have dusted the flour from her bibbed apron
and sat at the dining room table, the lace cloth
folded back, her glasses lying beside
the linen paper she'd taken from the sideboard.

She would have rubbed her eyes, trying to remember
what she did when she stirred the drops

and as she wrote, left out what everyone knew.
The linen paper's thin along the fold,

the edges flecked brown, but I'm typing the recipes,
printing in triplicate for my children and for me.
The copies are categorized and clean, the directions clear
and complete, but I miss the stains and tattered edges,

the search through cards and folded papers for the exact
recipe I need as if sight and scent are somehow stored
in ink, in crinkled paper, the smudges on the edge,
as if in the pattern of script, the writer lives.

Kitchen Tables

My son explored the attic and found the kitchen
table he knew would be a perfect size
for his apartment. I watched him scrape and clean
the streams of milk still dried beneath the leaves,
one glass of many spilled at the table
that was ours, and years before, his grandmother's.

"You can have it," she'd said. Tired of grandmother's
hand-me-downs, mother imagined a kitchen
she'd seen in magazines with a round table
in white. This was not the right size.
Once she ordered father to saw the leaves—
cherry that almost touched the floor. She cleaned

and covered the wood with oilcloth for easy cleaning.
None could recognize the table that had graced grandmother's
home, draped in crocheted lace, its leaves
outspread for guests who happened by her kitchen.
But now we fit around its altered size
to eat, our feet touching beneath the table.

Here we hurled words across the table.
Like rings in wood they've stayed, not to be cleaned
away like milk or cut like leaves to size.
Perhaps if we'd had the grander space of grandmother's,
they wouldn't have rung so loud inside the kitchen—
maybe they would not have made us want to leave.

When my husband stripped the varnish from the darkened leaves,
revealed the fire hidden in wood, the table
became our center for conversation and kitchen
meals, the children's paints and clay. When cleaned,
the cherry gleamed as it always had in grandmother's
time except for the leaves diminished size.

When we bought a bigger house, we found the size
gave space for the tiger maple we wanted with leaves

that almost touched the floor, the grace of grandmother's.
In the attic's heat and dark, the little table
deepened, like a white shirt packed away clean,
revealed its spots, waiting for another kitchen.

My son found its size was right, the perfect table.
He runs his hand along the leaves he cleaned.
Grandmother's table gleams in his kitchen.

Singing at the Table

My grandchildren sing while they eat
not a song with words, just a hum.
Their feet swing, keep a steady drum
beat against the chair legs or table.

Sometimes amid the clatter of knives and forks,
the voices of my son and husband beginning to rise
as ideas for waterproofing basements vie,
and the children's chorus humming beneath it all,

my husband snaps, "No singing at the table!"

One morning in the quiet of breakfast for four,
the children just starting softly to hum,
their grandfather just starting to drum
his eraser against the *Times'* puzzle,

the sun slid from behind the backyard maple,
touched the tops of heads bent over bowls,
and suddenly "Blue Skies," a song so old,
I had not heard in years came back,

and I danced around the table singing.

Then and Now

With My Grandmother

June found them on their knees. They had to creep
across the field careful not to crush
the berry carpet, ripe, red, lush.
The child soon learned the pressure to keep

between thumb and forefinger to free
the tiny berry, not lose its essence in a gush.
She matched her grandmother's rhythm, no rush.
Patience, she saw, is the way to reap

and slowly the empty pail will fill.
Even time seemed to creep in the hush of heat,
a canopy that hung over the flat, still
field. A bell might sound from a cow nearly asleep
in shade of fencerow trees. In sun
held by their work, woman and child were one.

With My Granddaughter

She looks at me in question, presses a blueberry
against her lips. I smile and nod my head.
We work our way around the bush: the very
bottom hers, the top mine. A thread

unravels. I am led into a labyrinth
where a child and her grandmother still live.
Once the empty pail had daunted me, no hint
that it would overflow. The day outlives

the hours spent in the sunfilled field,
stored like a jar of garnet in secret dark,
the scent of strawberries in sun, sealed.
On a morning when frost rimes tree bark,
we will tap our rich store,
savor a sweetness we had not known before.

V

Things Live After Us

For my friend R.V.

Things live after us:
the wheel rutted streets of Pompeii,
the fetal curve in hardened lava of child and dog,
the photograph of you posed at the ancient grindstone
to show your students how it once turned.
History teacher, you dealt in artifacts.
Your classroom walls papered with the past.
The framed Acropolis and Forum, reminders that
the White House and Pentagon unpeopled
will not tell our story.

The house is emptied.
Men worked in the dark.
The kitchen table, heavy with dishes, stands on the lawn.
The blue teapot saved on the back shelf,
its gold banding bright as your wedding day,
joins the cracked cups and chipped saucers white in the morning sun.
In the grass the cord of the kitchen clock dangles.
At the auctioneer's block,
books from the shelves next to your bed, boxed.
Soon strange eyes will scan the titles,
note your name printed on bookplates or scrawled inside covers,
and when the gavel pounds,
all the words you couldn't live without will scatter
like dandelion parachutes in the wind.

Identity

Rijksmuseum, Amsterdam

17th century Dutch whalers' caps from graves near Spitsbergen, Norway, opened in 1980

When their bodies were exhumed, the Dutchmen
still wore their knitted woolen caps.
Three hundred years undisturbed
in private dark. If they now could rise,
they'd be hailed by fellow whalers, recognized
by stripes and colors that individualized
the caps that clung to skulls that neither wife
nor mother could rightly claim for certain as her own.

Bundled against fierce cold, only their eyes
visible, they knew each other by green stripe,
or orange band knit by women whose hands
were powerless against storms they knew would come.
Aware each voyage could be their last,
the men packed wood to build their coffins,
perhaps some moss on which to rest their feet.
And when a body was prepared for burial in foreign soil,
a cap was drawn over the round of the nameless head,
the cap that set each man apart,
the cap that said, this is he.

The Saved

Anglo-Saxon lines- after Richard Wilbur

Attic trunks talked
          whispered, "Touch me.
Spring the latch,
          and lift the dome. Look."
Like Alice I listened,
          lifted weighty lids.
Once there lay lace,
          fragrance of lavender
Faint in the folds
          that unfanned between my fingers.
Beneath, bolts
          of cambric, banded by
Borders embroidered
          with a bride's bold initial
Pure white
          waiting, still.

*

Cast-off clothes
          cluttered the closet
Bent the boxes
          they balanced above
Pressed postcards
          preserved between pages
Their scrawled message
          strangely short.
Snapshots never sorted
          by subject or date
Black and white, some bent
          others blurry.
Though none were labeled,
          I knew some and named them
Noted the number

now anonymous.

*

A letter had lain long
                    in a leather
Folder frayed
                    and flattened.
Caught in its crease
                    a curl of hair
Brown as the braid
                    I held it beside.
"Dear daughter," it began,
                    "Diana drifted off
as we stood by
                    singing her favorite psalm.
We buried her
                    beside brother.
Keep faith.
                    Your loving father, Philip."

                              *

Such scattered segments
                    salvaged scraps
Like archaeological
                    artifacts
Defy death
                    dare us
To find in fragments
                    the full figure of a life
Press us for proof
                    of pattern and purpose.

A Hideaway

Not tins of toothpowder nor blue bottles
half-filled with liquid gone chalk, forgotten,
drew me. It was the smell of the woodshed.

No trace of ordinary must, the shed
perfumed the present, a vintage bottle
uncorked. Like pages of long forgotten

books, its fragrance brought back years forgotten.
The filled lamp on the table. The day shed
in a circle of light, the dark bottled.

The shed bottled me, the day forgotten.

Five Women

at the town book sale

From a folding table marked "fiction,"
I picked up *Middlemarch*, not to buy,
but simply to run my hand over, open
as if greeting an old friend. The genie

that rose was a name I knew, inked
in perfect Palmer on a card once marking
her place: to Louise from Chris, Florida,
Christmas, three decades ago.

Then both were my age, Louise, not dead,
her books still on her library shelves,
and Chris, years away from the nursing home
where she lives cocooned in a muffled world.

Growing up, I felt these women held the secret
to all that is printed in books. I loved the way
they talked grammatically, used words I'd never heard.
Chris was the mother of my best friend,

who made me promise not to tell
the times her mother was sent away.
When Chris came back, she sold shoes,
and chatted with customers in the family store.

Louise taught second grade and when she retired,
separated from her lumberjack husband,
then took trips to England and the continent.
On the December day the card arrived from Florida,

I picture Louise, wrapped in a wool afghan,
lost in Dorothea's world, but aware
that snow drifts just beyond the pane.
Chris's words, slipped between the pages, press into Eliot's.
Silent as remembered voices—the women.

Unfinished Quilts

"Fair Philomel, she but lost her tongue,
And in a tedious sampler sewed her mind."
William Shakespeare - *Titus Andronicus*

Great-grandmother set aside a room where quilters met
to fill each chest with quilts, thirteen the goal for girls—
Baby Block, Geese in Flight, Bear Claw, Mariner's Compass.
The one she left unfinished we stretched across a frame to quilt.

We watched our uneven tracks around shapes of fabric she'd stitched into
    pattern.
Poke the needle into the top through batting into back.
Then the trick to come up close to the stitch going down.
Concentration, no conversation, neck and back ached.

What of the women like one who stitched at her sampler's edge,
"By Mary Wilson, who hated every minute of it" ?
In lives that offered little choice, they kept their tongues.
Like Philomel, stitching in silence, each had her work to do.

Many of their quilts, plain, dark, serviceable, cut from scraps,
have not survived. Those that remain, saved for "good" or made
by women who died, their unused linens still stacked in chests,
wordless as their makers' joy in color, silent as their suppressed cries.

Gertrude

Sometimes I'd see her coming across the road
from her old white house higher on the hill than ours.
When Eric was alive, we'd shout, "Good morning,"
from our coffee on the porch (that's how close we are).

I hated to let her in—the smell of her unwashed hair
and cat piss that permeated the tattered sweater she'd thrown on
always lingered long after she'd gone
so I'd step outside and greet her on the walk.

She always had something to show me—pointing
with a yellow talon rimmed in black
to some bill that needed explanation. I'm bewildered
myself sometimes by words or the way numbers dance down a page

and wonder when I'm eighty-five if I'll know
what it all means so I tried to be patient and hold
my breath bending near knowing it was only
the start of a string of plaints she'd unreel.

A suspicion that somehow her television was
a device the Greybecks (the Snopses of the hill)
were using to spy on her or anger at the neighbor
boys' snooping in her barn or even at Eric for dying.

I'd listen as long as I could, then say
I was in the middle of supper and would she like some.
I couldn't ask her in so I'd cover a plate for her to carry
home, but one night I saw from the kitchen window

she'd sat right down on our back steps
and with her German shepherd watching every bite
ate the entire steak as if somehow she'd just remembered to eat.
In November we'd close up the house and go back to the city

but when I'd pass a woman huddled in a doorway
a shopping cart filled with her belongings,
I'd think of Gertrude and the animals alone in the house,
the snow drifting right up to the door.

I knew the farmer neighbor brought her groceries
and the mail from the end of the drive. But when he left,
the house was silent—the only other voice coming from the snow
of the flickering screen.

Women's Care

Georgina, Carrie, Jean

Jean's strength gets her half-way
from a chair so plumped with pillows, she's practically there,
but as she wavers between stand or fall, the chair
claims her. I fear one day

she'll miss, struggle on her back, legs in air
like a beetle, unable to right herself. Yet her way
of life for the past fifty years may,
at nearly ninety, mean survival. Her care

remains her own. I'm spared by her good genes or
luck, unlike my grandmother who had to feed
and dress her mother-in-law, her own needs
subsumed by the woman who developed an ulcerous sore

on a visit and never left, something you read
about in Chekhov or Balzac and, like lore,
don't believe happens any more
if it ever did. But fate like a seed

dormant in the dark suddenly sends a shoot
that vines around all it touches, strangles
to reach the light. So Grandmother combed the tangles,
pinned them in a bun, cleaned the festering foot

and guided great-grandmother to a chair angled
in the sun. Alone, she'd unbutton her dress, root
out the pins to loosen her hair and put
them under the rug. Hair dangling,

half-dressed, she'd sit and stare until
Grandmother appeared from sheets she'd wash and wring
by hand and hoist like sails every morning.
You'd think she'd take one look and want to kill

the old woman, but instead she'd sigh and bring
her to the kitchen where she could watch her fill
the stew pot to simmer, talking to her still
as if naming spices might ring

familiar in ears that did not seem to hear.
Three years she went on. When
Grandmother had a stroke at eighty-one,
twenty years later, Jean was there

to take her mother in, her apartment run
like a nursing home. No room to spare
Grandmother slept in the bed Jean's rarely
complaining husband left, to sleep in the one

spot remaining, the couch. But Jean soon
had her up, earrings snapped into place,
tucked in a chair to wheel around Macy's
then lunch in the third floor restaurant at noon.

Jean, now alone, can barely lace
her shoes to shuffle behind a walker from bedroom
to kitchen. She worries arthritic fingers will soon
not even bend at all, a phase

she won't be able to face childless and alone.
She is my aunt, but I am her daughter.
Yet she talks of the nursing home around the corner.
For now, she's content that I shop and visit or phone.

Powerless

Because they toss her like a doll, she cries.
They speak above her head as if her ears
no longer hear and she's no longer wise
enough to understand. They chide her fear
that her arthritic hands won't hold
her body steady above the yawning bowl,
the white tiles winking hard and cold.
She's prisoner here, she says, the nurses in control.

The child in me remembers the smell of soap,
a lathered cloth rubbed across my face,
my mother's grip that held me stronger than a rope,
my burning scalp, the air in mouth replaced
by soapy water, all trace of hope erased
that anyone would hear and grant me grace.

From Hulda Crooks' Journal

Hulda Crooks, the oldest woman to climb Mt. Fuji

When I was young, I wondered how I'd change
with age. I thought that growing old was growing
into someone else, but still I hoist
my pack on shoulders that are bent but strong
enough to carry food and gear, the burden
for the climb up Whitney when the weather's
good. The mountain's like a friend I need
to visit. I've learned its trees and shrubs by heart.
At first, I didn't know what lay ahead
but now the mountain's face is as familiar
as my own. No map can tell the roots
that rise above the ground, the pockets in rock
just right for hands to grip and haul the body
up, but like a friend whose moods I read,
I know the disposition of the land.

When people ask, do you still climb,
as if surprised I haven't tired yet,
I think of my retreat above the trees
where I watch hawks harness the breeze,
wings outstretched, carried motionless.
Like surfers propelled forward on waves, they float
until they feel the pull of earth, then pump
their way upward to catch another draft
to drift on. I bask on rocks, a lizard
not thinking of the climb ahead or back
or how the sun arcs the sky. I close
my eyes to the blue-gold day and the lakes
like shards of glass below and listen to the cry
of hawks and hear the beating of their wings.

Note: Between the ages of 65-92, Hulda Crooks climbed 14,000 foot Mt. Whitney
twenty-three times. At 91 years of age, she climbed Mt. Fuji.

"You need goals"

Hulda Crooks

Magnets hold the *Times* photo of Hulda Crooks
to my refrigerator door the way the children's A
papers carried home from school were once displayed.
Smiling from the top of Mt. Fuji, Hulda looks

unruffled by this climb in her ninety-first year.
Trying to discover her secret, sometimes I stare
at the picture, but her eyes are lost in her glasses' glare
and like mine her boots are ordinary gear.

In one hand she holds a staff, the other's raised
in victory salute. "You need goals," the caption reads.
The picture's weathered seven years of dust and needs
framing if I want it to last or is she part of a phase

I'll soon outgrow? I put her there the summer the house
emptied. I felt sorry for my husband—all those
bills and a wife suddenly wondering who she was.
Hulda seemed the antidote to help rouse

our spirits. I've grown used to the picture's being there,
so when I wash the door, I always put it back
not out of fear exactly, but maybe lack
of trust the refrigerator can handle being so bare.

Elephant Wisdom

for my daughter on the birth of her daughter

1
Females live together in families led
by a grandmother fifty or sixty years old
whose power lies in memories she holds
of unmapped trails once followed by the dead.
Sisters, daughters, calves, all needing to be fed,
pad along in convoy toward a distant goal,
eighty miles not straying from the fold,
bound, it seems, by some invisible thread.
Wisdom, learned and coursing in the blood or bred
in genes, carries the species from one generation
into the next as sometimes in words I've said
I hear Grandmother's echo as if choice had fled
into a cave where faint on walls, notations
read are records of family information.

2
I read records of family information
in the map of my newborn granddaughter's face
and in the melodies my cracking voice retraces,
lines, thought lost; for this life's creation
has recreated mine.   My grandmother's dedication
to song was family legend.   She sang as she laced
strips of crust over cherry pies or erased
tears, rocking until pain or fear's sedation
was sure.   No work more important, no obligation
greater.   "Rock and sing," I'd say.
Pressed to her resonant breast, I learned the relation
between life and song, and how love, the foundation
formed in simple acts of the everyday,
lives beyond words and body's decay.

3
What lives beyond words and body's decay
surprises.   My mother's love was hidden from me.

Once I believed if I vanished from sight like Persephone,
she would not search the earth, pray
for my return. But when in silence, clay
reclaimed her, wordless, I began to see
that cellar shelves filled with summer's bounty
she'd peeled, pitted, and pressed into jars were a way
of loving, like her cakes and breads, a stay
against life's confusions. When I married, she wrote
the family recipes in a book, perhaps to allay
the pain of separation. Even the day
we knew that death stood between us, her throat
could not release love, the words remote.

4
Her love was released, the words not remote,
the summer she took my daughter to her ceramic
class. She'd arrive early mornings to pick
her up for breakfast. Returning at evening, she'd quote
the child's words, amused. She seemed to note
with pleasure the very qualities she once was quick
to criticize as if through a lens made thick
by time, her vision was somehow clearer. She doted
on her granddaughter as they painted the final coat
on the blue frog soap dish. It still
sits on my sink, one of the gifts they toted
home that reminds me of her devotion
and how through love she was able to fulfill
what else might lie dormant, still.

5.
What else might lie dormant, still,
awakened at my daughter's birth. So when her cries
sent milk rushing in my breasts, I'd rise
confident the power my body held could still
her. And when her mouth fell slack, spilled
milk and her head dropped back, her sigh
might have been mine, so closely were we tied

by hungers only the other seemed able to fulfill.
I was the mother I'd always wanted until
then. She was the daughter I longed to be.
From the moment she was placed on my chest the cord still
pulsing, I felt my untrained hands were skilled
beyond knowing, directed not by me
but forces flowing in the blood suddenly free.

6.
Forces flowing in the blood were suddenly freed
when my daughter gave birth. As I stood at her side,
watching the head crown between her thighs,
I counted the moments until the child, free
threw hands wide in air that she
with a cry now breathed. Unbound, yet tied
to mother, grandmothers, and those who died,
absent but present within the three:
bud, branch, limb, the living tree.
Looking into my granddaughter's eyes, I could see
the same blue in which my self had drowned,
the woman saved on the shore, only me
in body. Now mother and daughter lost, found
that both had been child-transformed, bound.

7.
Both of us child-transformed are bound.
Like the elephants of Namibia that cross burning sands
to reach water, we follow blood's demands,
search for sustenance our forebears found.
After miles—suddenly a shimmer and the ground
gives way to a spring, a gift of the land
and all drink deep. Sometimes as I scan
the face caught by the nightlight, astounded,
I see Grandmother. If only the sound
of her voice spoke clear and again I could hear
the words she would whisper that could drown
fear. Then I would draw their comfort around

our shoulders as she did who was not a seer
but a woman who through listening had learned to hear.

Daughter, our power lies in memories we hold
and in melodies, thought lost, our voice retraces.
The day that death stands between us our throats
will release love, the words not remote.
And forces in the blood will flow, suddenly freed
into the bud, branch, the living tree.
The ground will give way and we'll drink deep.

Acknowledgments

Grateful acknowledgment is made to the following journals in which these poems have appeared:

A Christmas Collection : "The Christmas Village" published by July Literary Press

Adirondac : "East Hill View," "On His Own," "Before acid rain"

Appalachia: "The Search"

Architrave : "A Lost Duchess"

Array : "Not Like Dick and Jane"

Blueline : "The Homestead," "Going Home," "Connected"

Broadkill Review: "Unfinished Quilts," "The Saved," "Memorials"

California State Poetry Quarterly : "A Marriage"

Child of My Child: "Now a Mother"

Cyclamensandswords.com "Vultures," "Land of the Heart," "In the Silk Factory," "Then and Now," "With Him"

Earth's Daughters: "Recipes," "Things Live After Us"

Ekphrasis: "Fox Hunt," "Bright Light at Russell's Corners"

Exit 13: "Sahara Dark," "Varanasi, Night Ride," "Obsolescence"

Forgotten Women: "From Hulda Crooks' Journal"

Hellas : "Comfort in Stone," "Promise of Flowers"

Joys of the Table: An Anthology of Culinary Verse: "Making Bread with Jonathan," "Recipes"

Knowing Stones: Poems of Exotic Places: "Horus' Eye"

Love is Ageless, Stories about Alzheimer's Disease: "A Marriage"

Miramar: "Five Women"

Newark Review: "Civility," "Kitchen Tables"

Off Line, An Anthology of New Jersey Poets: "Mysteries"

Outerbridge: "Windfalls," "Tattooed"

Romantics Quarterly: "Betrayed"

Salonika: "Women's Care," "Making Bread with Jonathan," "Dream of Spain"

Slab : "The Beginning"

The Comstock Review: "Powerless"

The English Journal : "Emblems"

The Final Lilt of Songs: "Lost World," "The Gathering of Women"

The MacGuffin : "Mother and Child," "You Need Goals"

The Kerf: "All About Crows"

The Sow's Ear Contest finalist : "From Hulda Crooks' Journal"

U.S.1 Worksheets: "Storm," "Ex Voto," "Tiger Hour," "The Dark," "With My Father," "Identity," "Singing at the Table"

Voices of Israel 2015: "At Auschwitz, In a Display Case," "Unclaimed"

Wavelength: "Gertrude"

Whetstone: "She Preserves," "In the Artist's Hand"

Xanadu: "On Our Anniversary"

Some poems were published in *Comfort in Stone*, a chapbook, Finishing Line Press, 2014

Some poems were published in *Things Live After*, a chapbook, Finishing Line Press, 2018

With gratitude to Marie Ponsot, mentor, friend, from whom I learned the art of listening.

Special thanks to Emily, Deena, Charlotte, Molly, and the XY Poets.

Carol Nolde and her husband live in Westfield, New Jersey, where she taught English and creative writing and for many years was an associate editor for *Merlyn's Pen*, a national magazine of teenage writers.

She and her family spend part of each year in Sullivan County, New York, in the foothills of the Catskills, where her ancestors settled in the early 19th century. She grew up in the house her great-grandparents built on the land cleared for farming by her great-great grandparents, immigrants from Ireland. The photograph on the cover (c. 1901) is of Georgina Taylor Stephenson, Nolde's great grandmother, and her son James, Nolde's grandfather, from whom she developed a deep appreciation of her heritage. Nolde's poetry reflects a life steeped in family history and the history of the region.

Her poems have appeared in many publications including the anthologies *Knowing Stones: Poems of Exotic Places,* the second edition of *Love Is Ageless-Stories About Alzheimer's Disease, Child of My Child, Joys of the Table,* and *Forgotten Women.* She is the author of the chapbook *Comfort in Stone* (Finishing Line Press, 2014) and the chapbook *Things Live After* (Finishing Line Press, 2018).